Now S

in Y

Living Room

by Lisa Cocca

HOUGHTON MIFFLIN BOSTON

PHOTOGRAPHY CREDITS: Cover © Schenectady Museum; Hall of Electrical History Foundation/Corbis; tp © POPPERFOTO/Alamy; 3 © Schenectady Museum; Hall of Electrical History Foundation/Corbis; 4, 5 © Bettmann/Corbis; 6. © SSPL/The Image Works; 7 © Schenectady Museum; Hall of Electrical History Foundation/Corbis; 8 © POPPERFOTO/ Alamy; 10, 11 © Associated Press.

Printed in China

ISBN-13: 978-0-547-02171-3
ISBN-10: 0-547-02171-2

14 15 16 17 0940 19 18 17 16
4500569761

Table of Contents

An Exciting Invention

Imagine that your family is at home, watching a football game on television. A player throws the ball for a touchdown and you can see every moment, as if you were there.

Now imagine that it's 1939. Another family is watching television. This is the first time they have even seen a television set! They are at the World's Fair in New York City, which was just about the only place where you could watch television in 1939.

The televisions at the 1939 World's Fair looked similar to this one.

A company called RCA showed home television sets with six-inch-wide screens at the 1939 New York World's Fair.

Someone pushes a button on the television set. There were no remotes back then! A picture slowly appears. It is President Franklin Roosevelt and the picture is in black and white. Even though it is hard to see through the static on the screen, no one leaves the room. Watching television for the first time is thrilling for each of them.

Television Is Born

In 1925, Charles Jenkins made the first television in the United States. The first sets worked with a motor that turned a metal disk. A neon tube sat behind the disk and gave off light. The pictures were not very clear, and the first screen was only one inch wide! Still, people were fascinated, and Jenkins's work generated lots of interest. Soon afterward, a man named Philo Farnsworth invented a better television.

Philo Farnsworth is known as the "Father of Television." He invented the first electronic television.

Early televisions had picture tubes inside them that looked like this.

This new-and-improved version of the television used a special electronic part called a picture tube. The sets needed bright, hot lights to work. However, the pictures were still not as clear as the ones you see today.

People kept working to make the television better. They changed the picture tubes. Within a couple of years, television sets improved greatly. Still, few people but inventors had television sets.

The Golden Age of Television

In 1941, the National Broadcasting Corporation (NBC) began to air programs to the public. The companies that made televisions also found cheaper ways to make the sets. They lowered the cost so that more people could buy them.

People had loved listening to ballgames on the radio. By the late 1940s, they could watch their teams on television.

As television sets became more affordable, stations began creating entertaining programs to draw new fans. They did this by showing a children's program at eight o'clock in the evening. The children were still awake, so the family could watch the show together. Later at night, the programming switched to dramas that adults could enjoy. Television stations earned money by allowing companies to advertise in commercials.

The adults stayed awake to watch teleplays created especially for the television audience. Many of these were live shows, and viewers were able to see all of the actors' mistakes. Viewers enjoyed watching these dramas.

Some of the popular television programs during the 1950s included *I Love Lucy*, *The Ed Sullivan Show*, and *Lassie*. As television shows became more popular, more people bought televisions. In 1950, fewer than one in ten homes in America had a television set, but by 1960, more than eight out of ten homes had one.

In Living Color

The first color television sets were invented in 1946. Color televisions changed over time. At first, a color wheel sat in front of the picture tube. Later, a three-color tube replaced the wheel. In 1951, people watched color programs for the first time.

During this period, television broadcasting companies were making their transmitting stations more and more powerful.

On July 20, 1969, Americans watched Neil Armstrong take the first steps on the moon.

Early color television sets were expensive.

People in California wanted to use television to promote their state and get more people to come visit. They got their wish on New Year's Day, 1954. People across America watched the Rose Bowl Parade on television. If they watched on a color set, they were also lucky enough to see the colorful flowers that gave the parade its name.

Five years later, in 1959, a weekly show began to air in color. Two years later, "Walt Disney's Wonderful World of Color" aired for the first time. By 1966, one network switched all of its new programs to color. Color television was here to stay.

Today and Tomorrow

Today, television is a big part of American life. It is now available on over one hundred channels. Now you can watch your favorite sports shows on a 40-inch plasma screen that makes you feel like you are at the game.

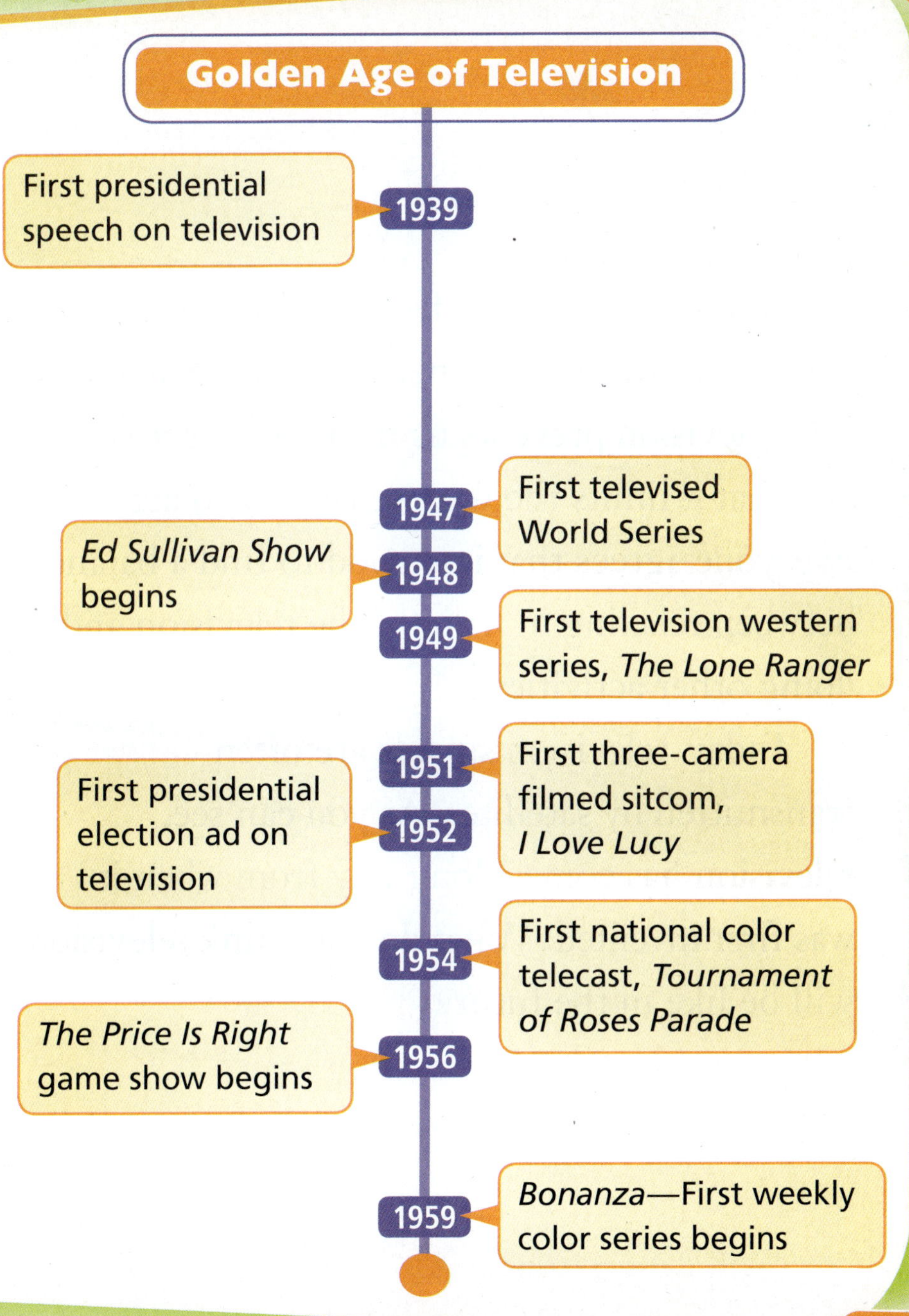
Golden Age of Television
1939
First presidential speech on television
1947
First televised World Series
1948
Ed Sullivan Show begins
1949
First television western series, *The Lone Ranger*
1951
First three-camera filmed sitcom, *I Love Lucy*
1952
First presidential election ad on television
1954
First national color telecast, *Tournament of Roses Parade*
1956
The Price Is Right game show begins
1959
Bonanza—First weekly color series begins

While many people feel television is a wonderful invention, others disagree. Some feel that television prevents us from being active and that it limits the way we think and act. Everyone agrees that it is good to find a balance between relaxing in front of the television and doing other activities.

Today, television signals are often transmitted by satellites. As you can see, television has come a long way from when it was first invented. What do you think television will be like in the future?

Responding

TARGET SKILL **Fact and Opinion** What facts and opinions does the author provide in this book? Copy and complete the chart below.

Fact	Opinion
The first color television sets were invented in 1946. ?	It is good to find a balance between watching television and doing other things. ?

Write About It

Text to World Do you think that television affects the way you and your friends think, behave, or dress? Write a paragraph in which you describe specific ways that television affects you or your friends.

TARGET VOCABULARY

advertise	generated
angles	jolts
critics	promote
entertaining	target
focus	thrilling

TARGET SKILL **Fact and Opinion** Decide if an idea can be proved or if it is a feeling or belief.

TARGET STRATEGY **Summarize** Briefly tell the important parts of the text in your own words.

GENRE **Informational Text** gives facts and examples about a topic.